HAL•LEONARD
INSTRUMENTAL
PLAY-ALONG

CLASSICAL SOLOS
FOR
FLUTE
VOLUME 2

T0079139

The enclosed audio CD is also a CD-ROM and includes:
Piano accompaniment for each solo in PDF format for printing.
Tempo Adjustment Software for use with most PC or Mac computers. Instructions included.

ISBN 978-1-4803-5115-8

HAL•LEONARD®
CORPORATION
7777 W. BLUEMOUND RD. P.O. BOX 13819 MILWAUKEE, WI 53213

Visit Hal Leonard Online at
www.halleonard.com

LARGO
from *Xerxes*

GEORGE FRIDERIC HANDEL
Arranged by PHILIP SPARKE

flute

Largo (♩ = 68)

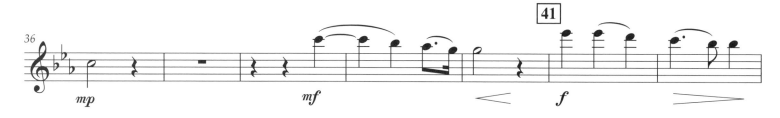

SONGS MY MOTHER TAUGHT ME

3

from *Gypsy Songs*

ANTONÍN DVORÁK
Arranged by PHILIP SPARKE

Flute

Andante con moto
(♩ = 108)

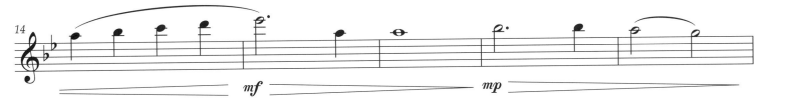

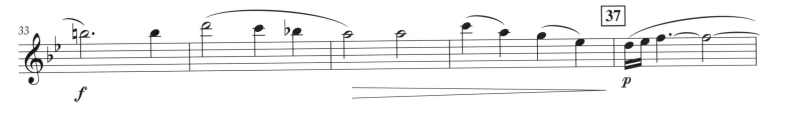

00121134

MINUET NO. 2
from *Notebook for Anna Magdalena Bach*

Flute

Attributed to CHRISTIAN PEZOLD
Arranged by PHILIP SPARKE

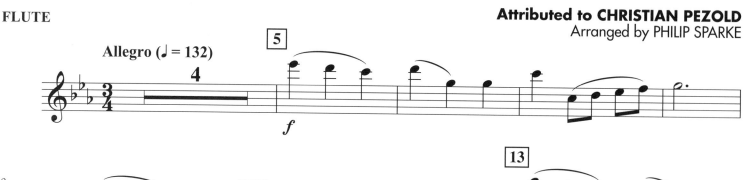

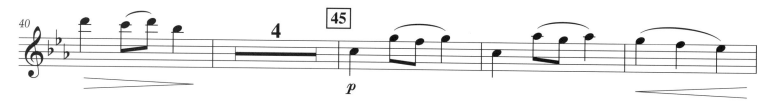

LA CINQUANTAINE
from *Two Pieces for Cello and Piano*

JEAN GABRIEL-MARIE
Arranged by PHILIP SPARKE

Flute

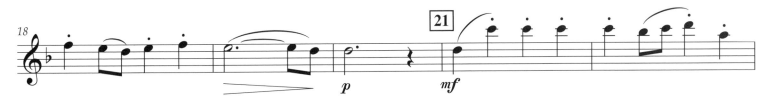

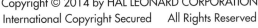

00121134

SEE, THE CONQUERING HERO COMES

from *Judas Maccabeus*

GEORGE FRIDERIC HANDEL
Arranged by PHILIP SPARKE

FLUTE

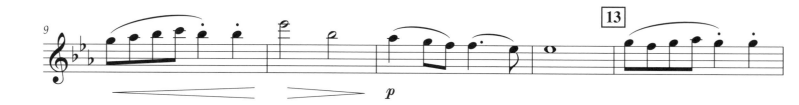

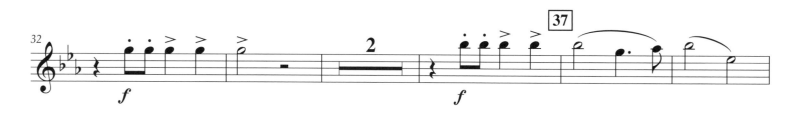

SONATINA
Op. 36, No. 1

MUZIO CLEMENTI
Arranged by PHILIP SPARKE

FLUTE

Allegro (♩ = 88)

00121134

8

SERENATA
from *String Quartet, Op. 3, No. 5*

FRANZ JOSEPH HAYDN
Arranged by PHILIP SPARKE

Flute

Andante cantabile (♩ = 96)

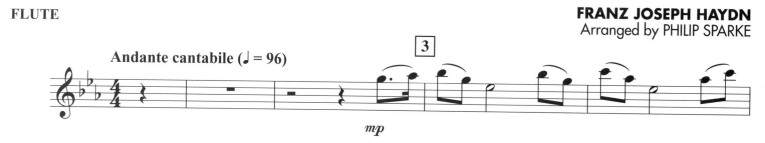

TAMBOURIN
from *Second Suite in E Minor*

JEAN-PHILIPPE RAMEAU
Arranged by PHILIP SPARKE

FLUTE

Vivo (♩ = 104)

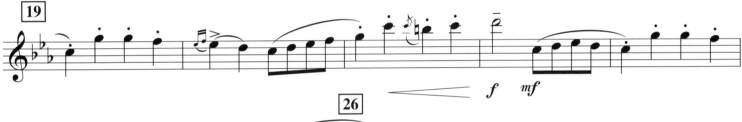

rall.

00121134

WALTZ
from *Album for the Young*

PYOTR ILYICH TCHAIKOVSKY
Arranged by PHILIP SPARKE

FLUTE

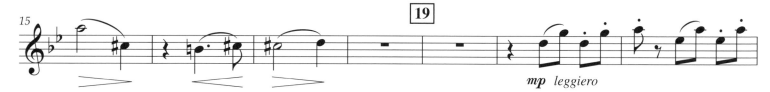

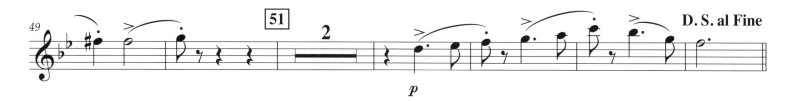

00121134

SONATINA
from *Six Pieces, Op. 3*

CARL MARIA VON WEBER
Arranged by PHILIP SPARKE

FLUTE

Moderato e con amore
($\bullet$ = 120)

GAVOTTE
from *Paride ed Elena*

CHRISTOPH GLUCK/arr. JOHANNES BRAHMS
Arranged by PHILIP SPARKE

Flute

SONATA
Op. 118, No. 1

ROBERT SCHUMANN
Arranged by PHILIP SPARKE

FLUTE

00121134

SERENADE
from *Schwanengesang, D.957*

FRANZ SCHUBERT
Arranged by PHILIP SPARKE

FLUTE

00121134

SONATINA
Anh. 5, No. 1

LUDWIG VAN BEETHOVEN
Arranged by PHILIP SPARKE

Flute

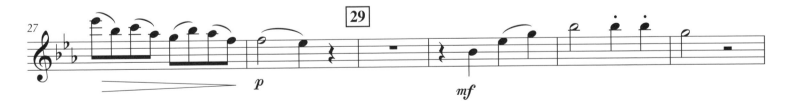

BOURRÉE
from *Flute Sonata, HWV 363b*

GEORGE FRIDERIC HANDEL
Arranged by PHILIP SPARKE

FLUTE

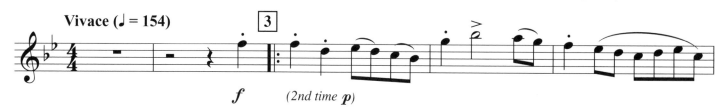